T0042171

Pebble® Plus

Life Around the World

Transportation in Many Cultures

Revised Edition

by Martha E. H. Rustad
Consulting Editor: Gail Saunders-Smith, PhD

CAPSTONE PRESS
a capstone imprint

Pebble Plus is published by Capstone Press,
1710 Roe Crest Drive, North Mankato, Minnesota 56003.
www.mycapstone.com

Copyright © 2008, 2016 by Capstone Press, a Capstone imprint. All rights reserved.
No part of this publication may be reproduced in whole or in part, or stored in a retrieval system, or transmitted in any form or by any means, electronic, mechanical, photocopying, recording, or otherwise, without written permission of the publisher. For information regarding permission, write to Capstone Press, 1710 Roe Crest Drive, North Mankato, Minnesota 56003.

Library of Congress Cataloging-in-Publication Data is available on the Library of Congress website.
ISBN: 978-1-5157-4292-0 (hardback)
ISBN: 978-1-5157-4241-8 (paperback)
ISBN: 978-1-5157-4361-3 (ebook pdf)

Editorial Credits
Sarah L. Schuette, editor; Kim Brown, book designer; Alison Thiele, set designer; Wanda Winch, photo researcher

Photo Credits
Capstone Studio: Karon Dubke, 9; Getty Images: Opus/a.collectionRF, 7; Shutterstock: Adisa, Cover, Anton_Ivanov, 21, cowardlion, 11, gary718, 1, imagestockdesign, 13, Ivan Cholakov, 17, Melissa King, 19, thieury, 5, Thorsten Rust, 15

Note to Parents and Teachers

The Life around the World set supports national social studies standards related to culture and geography. This book describes and illustrates transportation in many cultures. The images support early readers in understanding the text. The repetition of words and phrases helps early readers learn new words. This book also introduces early readers to subject-specific vocabulary words, which are defined in the Glossary section. Early readers may need assistance to read some words and to use the Table of Contents, Glossary, Read More, Internet Sites, and Index sections of the book.

Printed and bound in the USA.
082017 010708R

Table of Contents

Transportation 4
Going to School 6
Going Other Places 14
On the Go! 20

Glossary 22
Read More 23
Internet Sites 23
Index 24

Transportation

People travel
in every culture.
Let's see how other people
around the world travel.

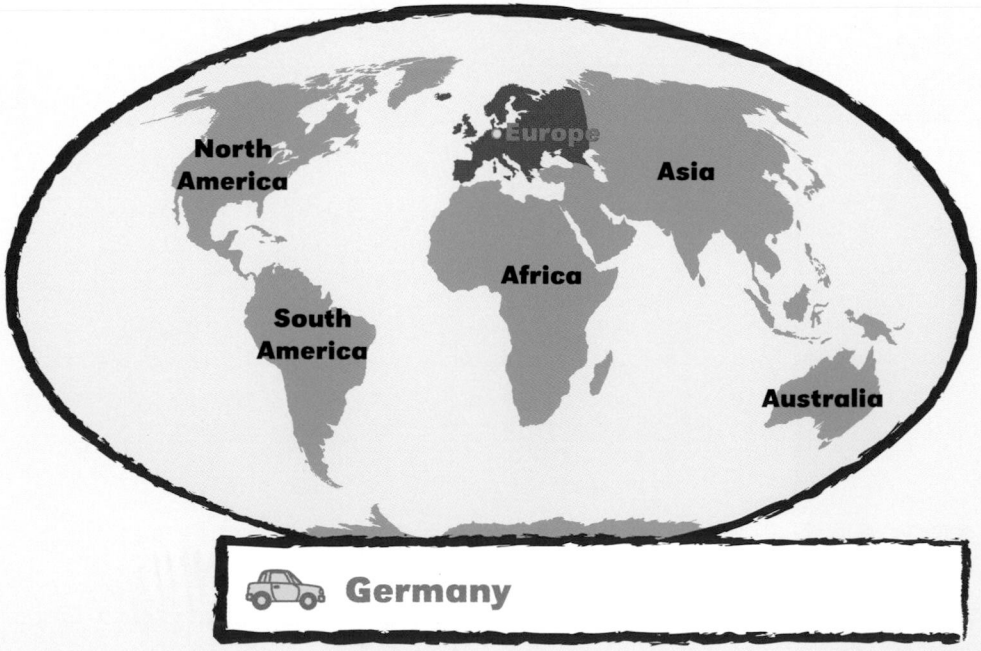

Going to School

These girls in China
walk to school.

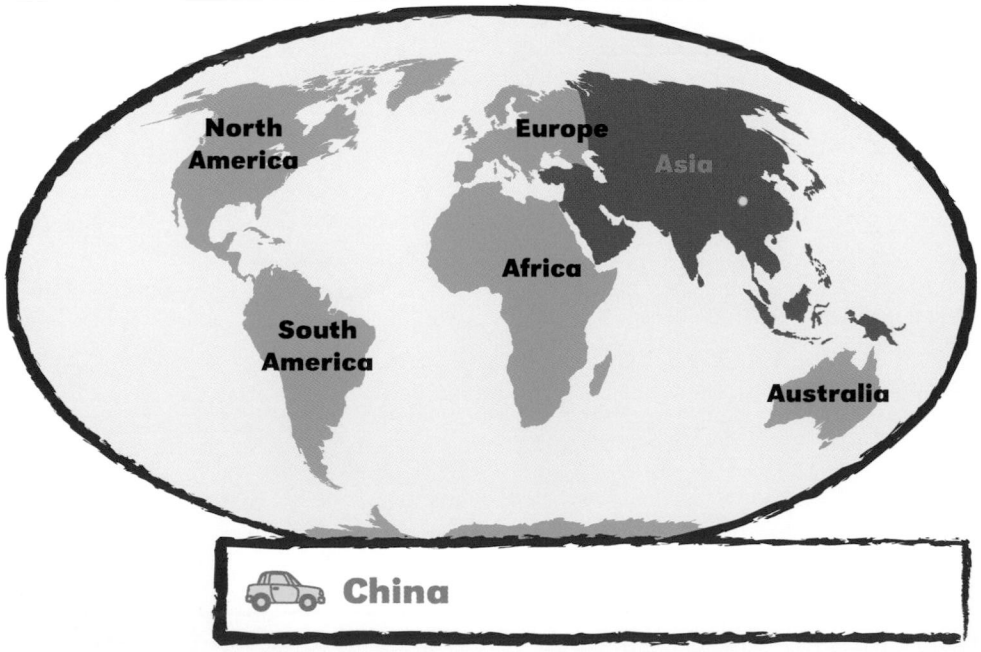

These boys in
the United States
ride a bus to school.

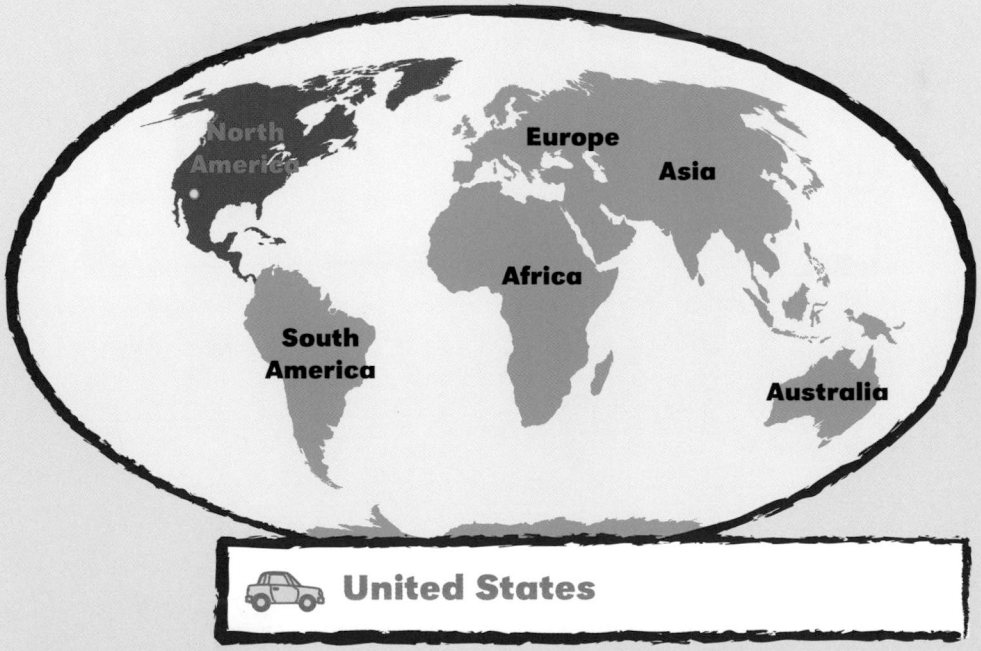

These girls in Japan
ride a train to school.

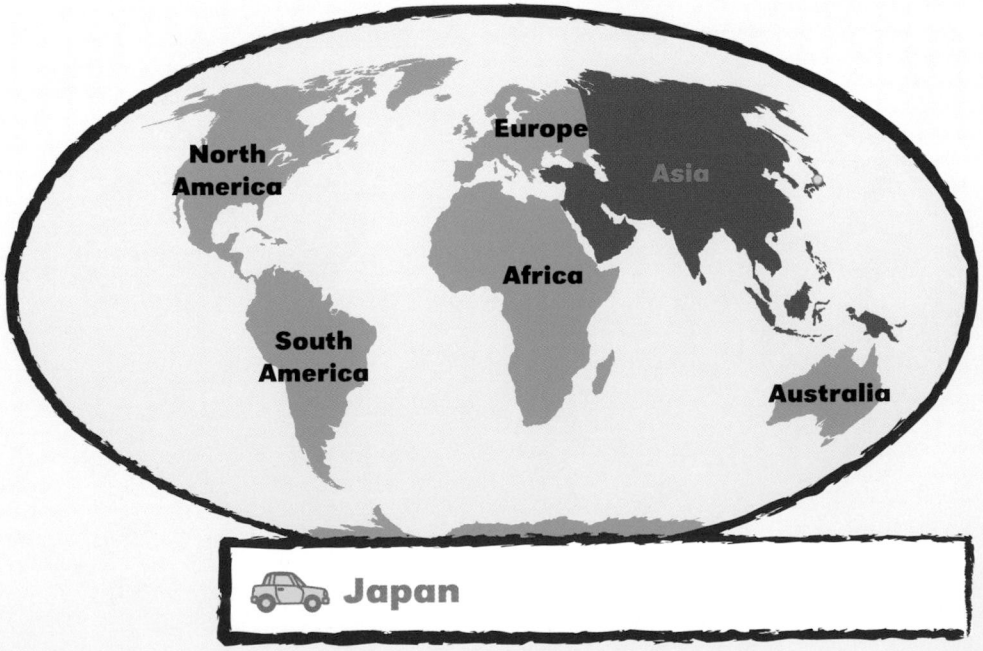

DODA
時間テレビ

These kids in Cambodia
paddle boats to get
to their floating school.

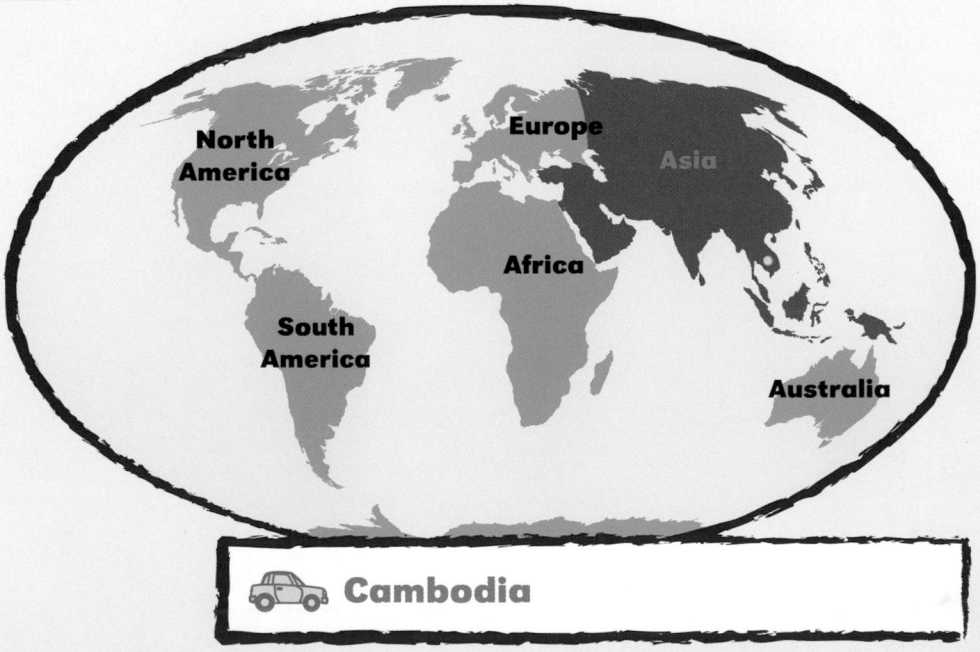

Going Other Places

People in Australia
ride the monorail.

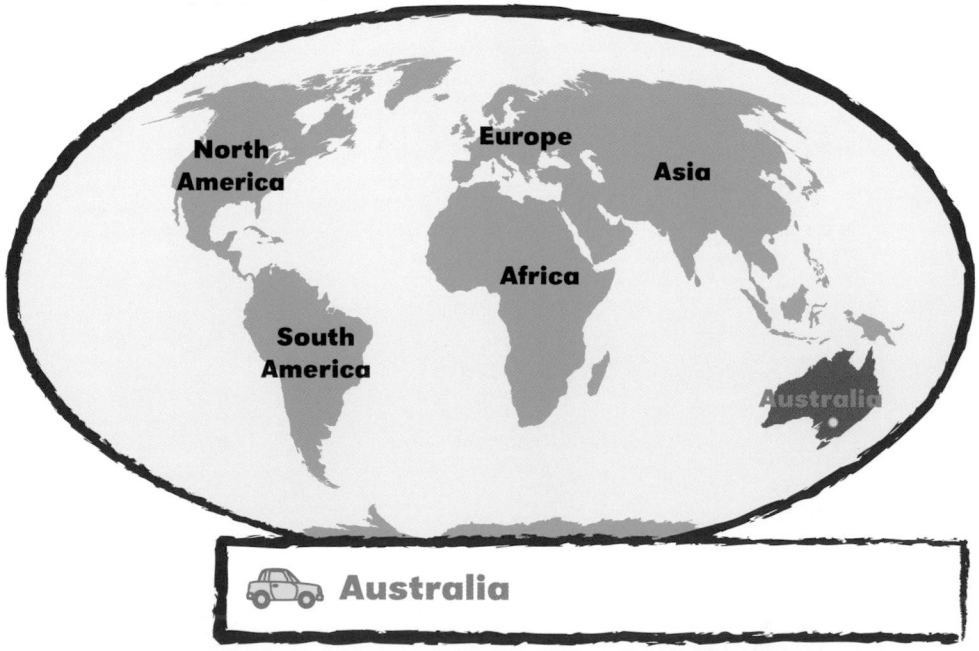

$49 - $200
Gap

Travelers in Bolivia
take an airplane
to another country.

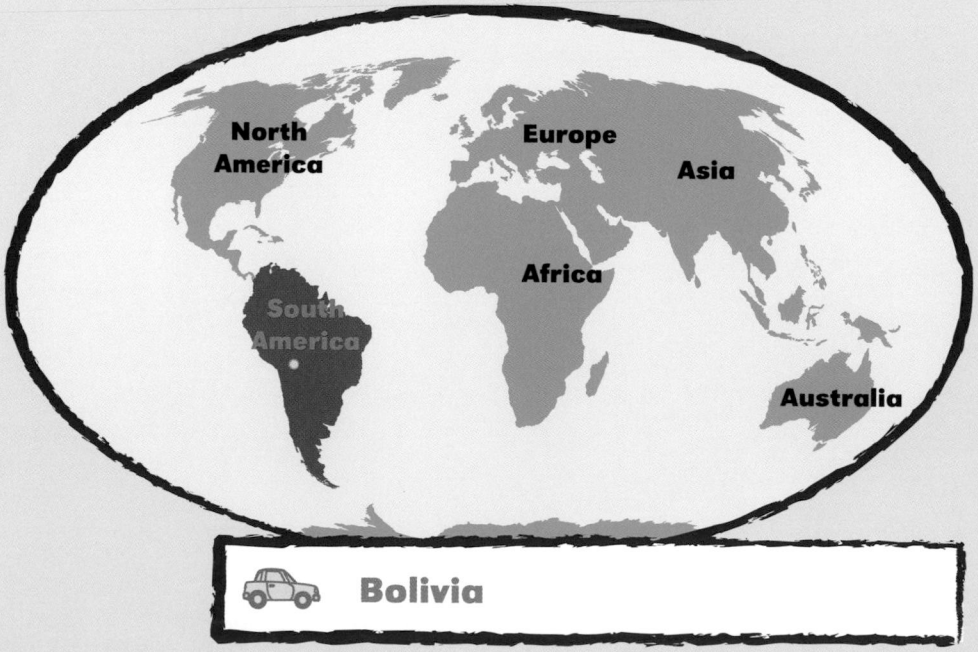

LAB
www.labairlines.com.bo
BOEING 727-200
CP-1367
LLOYD AEREO BOLIVIANO

A boy in Canada
rides a snowmobile.

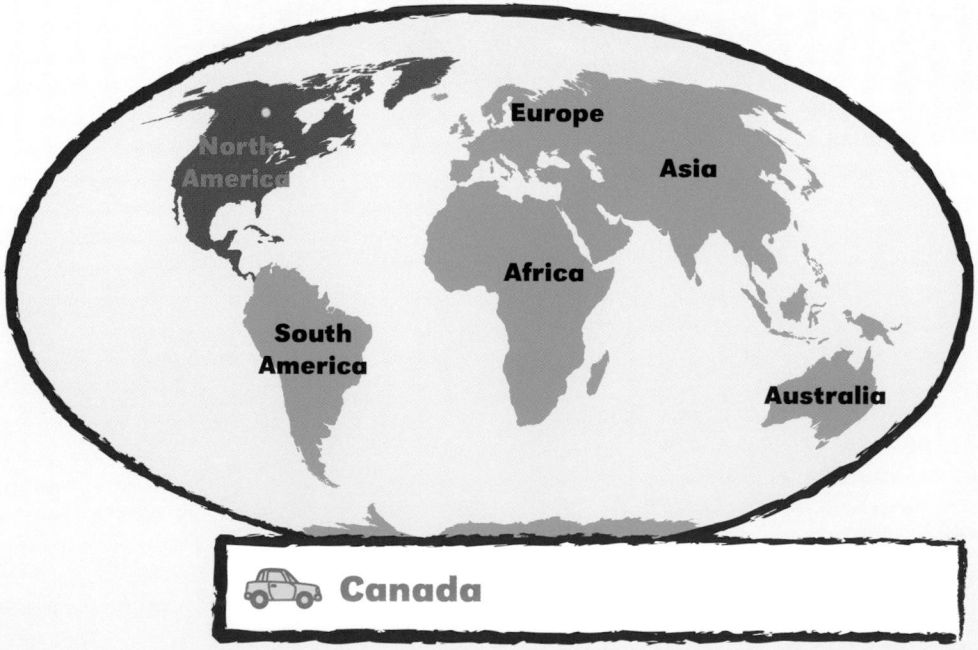

On the Go!

Around the world,
people ride buses, bicycles,
and animals.
How will you travel today?

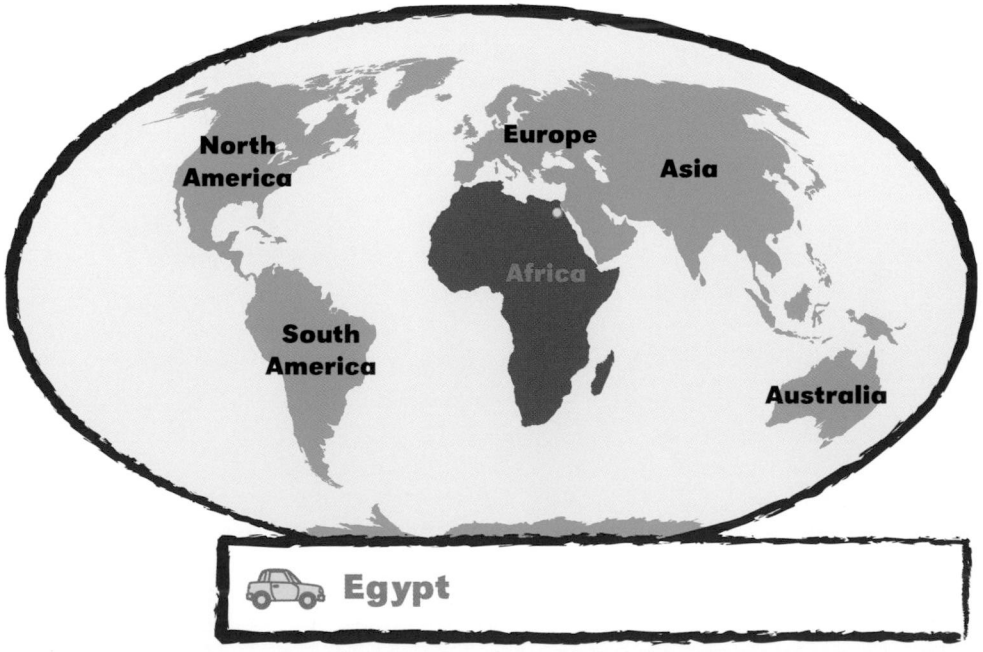

Glossary

culture — the way of life, ideas, customs, and traditions of a group of people

monorail — a train that runs on one rail, usually high off the ground

paddle — to push through the water with an oar

snowmobile — a vehicle with skis used to travel over snow

travel — to go from one place to another

Read More

Guin, Valerie. *On the Move.* One World. North Mankato, Minn.: Smart Apple Media, 2006.

Mattern, Joanne. *Transportation.* Yesterday and Today. San Diego: Blackbirch Press, 2004.

Weber, Rebecca. *How We Travel.* Spyglass Books. Minneapolis: Compass Point Books, 2004.

Internet Sites

FactHound offers a safe, fun way to find Internet sites related to this book. All of the sites on FactHound have been researched by our staff.

Here's how:

1. Visit *www.facthound.com*
2. Choose your grade level.
3. Type in this book ID **1429617446** for age-appropriate sites. You may also browse subjects by clicking on letters, or by clicking on pictures and words.
4. Click on the **Fetch It** button.

FactHound will fetch the best sites for you!

Index

airplanes, 16
animals, 20
Australia, 14
bicycles, 20
boats, 12
Bolivia, 16
buses, 8, 20
Cambodia, 12
Canada, 18
China, 6
cultures, 4
Japan, 10
monorails, 14
school, 6, 8, 10, 12
snowmobiles, 18
trains, 10
United States, 8
walking, 6

Word Count: 89
Grade: 1
Early-Intervention Level: 18